GENERATION CORAZON

Abhijit Naskar is the twenty-first century Neuroscientist whose contributions in Cognitive and Behavioral Neuroscience have helped the world tackle the issues of systemic racism, prejudice, hate, extremism, discrimination and biases more effectively. As an untiring advocate of mental health and universal acceptance, he became a beloved best-selling author all over the world with his very first book "The Art of Neuroscience in Everything". With his pioneering ventures into the Neuropsychology of beliefs and biases, he has hugely contributed in the eradication of religious and cultural differences in our world, for which he is popularly hailed as the humanitarian scientist, who takes the human civilization in the path of sweet general harmony.

GENERATION CORAZON

Nationalism is Terrorism

ABHIJIT NASKAR

Also by Abhijit Naskar

The Art of Neuroscience in Everything
Your Own Neuron: A Tour of Your Psychic Brain
The God Parasite: Revelation of Neuroscience
The Spirituality Engine
Love Sutra: The Neuroscientific Manual of Love
Homo: A Brief History of Consciousness
Neurosutra: The Abhijit Naskar Collection
Autobiography of God: Biopsy of A Cognitive Reality
Biopsy of Religions: Neuroanalysis towards Universal
Tolerance
Prescription: Treating India's Soul
What is Mind?
In Search of Divinity: Journey to The Kingdom of Conscience
Love, God & Neurons: Memoir of a scientist who found
himself by getting lost
The Islamophobic Civilization: Voyage of Acceptance
Neurons of Jesus: Mind of A Teacher, Spouse & Thinker
Neurons, Oxygen & Nanak
The Education Decree
Principia Humanitas
The Krishna Cancer
Rowdy Buddha: The First Sapiens
We Are All Black: A Treatise on Racism
The Bengal Tigress: A Treatise on Gender Equality
Either Civilized or Phobic: A Treatise on Homosexuality
Wise Mating: A Treatise on Monogamy
Illusion of Religion: A Treatise on Religious
Fundamentalism
The Film Testament
Human Making is Our Mission: A Treatise on Parenting
I Am The Thread: My Mission
7 Billion Gods: Humans Above All
Lord is My Sheep: Gospel of Human
Morality Absolute
A Push in Perception
Let The Poor Be Your God
Conscience over Nonsense
Saint of The Sapiens
Time to Save Medicine
Fabric of Humanity
Build Bridges not Walls: In the name of Americana
The Constitution of The United Peoples of Earth

Lives to Serve Before I Sleep
When Humans Unite: Making A World Without Borders
All For Acceptance
Monk Meets World
Mission Reality
Citizens of Peace: Beyond The Savagery of Sovereignty
Operation Justice: To Make A Society That Needs No Law
See No Gender
The Gospel of Technology
Every Generation Needs Caretakers: The Gospel of
Patriotism
Aşkanjali: The Sufi Sermon
Mad About Humans: World Maker's Almanac
Revolution Indomable
When Call The People: My World My Responsibility
No Foreigner Only Family
Hurricane Humans: Give me accountability, I'll give you
peace
Ain't Enough to Look Human
Servitude is Sanctitude
Time To End Democracy: The Meritocratic Manifesto
I Vicdansaadet Speaking: No Rest Till The World is Lifted
Boldly Comes Justice: Sentient not Silent
Good Scientist: When Science and Service Combine
Sleepless for Society
Neden Türk: The Gospel of Secularism
Martyr Meets World: To Solve The Hard Problem of
Inhumanity
The Shape of A Human: Our America Their America
When Veins Ignite: Either Integration or Degradation
Heart Force One: Need No Gun to Defend Society
Solo Standing on Guard: Life Before Law

DEDICATION

This book is dedicated to Alan Alda

CONTENTS

1. The Secret to Life

Corazón mine, don't you dare beat for me! Beat for those who have lost all melody. That'll be the fulfillment of my life. The unfortunate reality is, there are more fake hearts in the world than there are stars in the sky. Real heart is one that beats for others, and that which beats only for the self, is no human heart to begin with.

It is extremely easy to be born, live and die only for the self, all animal do that, what's human is to be born for others, live for others and die for others. When the eternal winter comes, there'll be only one question in front of your eyes - what have you left behind for others?

Remember, to move from darkness to light, from selfishness to selflessness, is what defines human life. And in fact, this is the true evolution from non-existence to existence. So, wake up o selfless soldier and give all to the world - and the world will be yours. Absolute and utter submission at the feet of the helpless, is the secret to life.

I don't want the world, I already have it. I want you to have it, the whole world, not just a fraction of land imprisoned by borders. And if you want the world, you have to make your heart big as the world first.

Remember, annihilation is far better than a vegetative existence. If you don't feel for others, if you don't feel for the world, if your blood doesn't boil at the sight of their suffering, then you are not living. If injustice sets you on fire, if discrimination sets you on fire, if disparities set you on fire, then only there is life in your veins - if not, then no matter how well-versed you are in pompous ideologies and philosophical and scientific theories, you are just a good-looking caveman.

2. Miracle Human (The Sonnet)

Miracle Human
(The Sonnet)

Turning water into wine is no miracle,
It just means you are high on something.
Real miracle is to share your last drop,
With someone who is suffering.
To heal and to help are the highest miracle,
Even if it requires the self to be sacrificed.
A mortal who bears agony for others,
Is the real miracle personified.
So wake up and work O Miracle Human,
Rush to the helpless as monsoon rain.
Cast yourself at the feet of the forgotten,
There is nothing more noble and humane.
Prayers don't work for there's no merciful almighty.
Answer to all prayers is a human practicing humanity.

3. Life is Not The Word

First of all, life cannot be defined with words. Secondly, if it must be defined, it can only be done with simple words. Simpler the words, the more meaningful they are. And there is nothing more meaningful than kindness, there is nothing more meaningful than reason, there is nothing more meaningful than accountability.

To witness accountability, you must become accountability - to witness reason, you must become reason - to witness kindness, you must become kindness. Whatever we are, so is the world, for the world is but a reflection of us.

In one of my early works, I had said, self is all, that is, all that there is in the world is but a reflection of the self. Therefore, all reform starts with the self. Now here the question that rises is, how do I reconcile this with another common statement of mine, where I ask you to wipe out the self to see real reform!

And the answer is, this is where words fall short. If you can go beyond the limitations of the words, you'd realize that in wiping out the self for the benefit of others, that self comes back to you hundred times larger, stronger and happier.

So you see, the very divide between the self and society is the problem here. Erase that division and all will be well with society, for once you erase that divide between the self and society, there is no longer any difference between the reform of the self and the reform of society.

So, when I say, self is all, it's not the puny self of the selfish animal, rather it is the self big enough to engulf the whole world. Society needs policy so long as the self is separate from it. Once the self and society become one, individual accountability takes over, and there is no longer any need for policy or law of any kind.

4. Sonnet of Chemical Reality

14

Sonnet of Chemical Reality

The universe is our reflection,
We are the reflection of the universe.
What is inside is also outside,
What is outside is also inside of us.
No reality exists without human control,
Reality outside our control is imagination.
Mental chemicals produce all reality,
All can be altered with mindful action.
Mind is mightier than muscle,
Kindness is braver than cruelty.
All reform is born of mental chemicals,
Reform yourself and there'll be universality.
Truth beyond perception is futile speculation.
Let's focus on life and improve human condition.

5. Expand Beyond Yourself

18

One of the fundamental acts of accountability is to conquer one's biases and prejudices. But this act is not a one-time endeavor, rather it is life itself, for the mind is never without biases and prejudices - its very purpose is to produce biases and prejudices that constitute most of what we call perception. Therefore, you must be aware of your biases and prejudices every step of the way, but not in insecurity, rather in a jolly and lively manner. Remember, it's growth that defines life, not rigidity.

Let me elaborate this further with an example of our time. A police officer oblivious to their errors and shortcomings is no different from the Gestapo. Such police may be suitable in Nazi Germany, Imperialist Britain, Confederate America or the Amazon jungle, but they have no place in a society of civilized beings.

In fact, the way things are going, it wouldn't be wrong to say, America is the land of liberty for white people, but for the people of color it's (almost) Nazi Germany. And one civilized government cannot change that, for people hold the reins of reform, not politicians.

The only way forward is realization - realization of one's own biases - realization of one's own shortcomings - realization of one's own predominant assumptions. All reform is born of realization - no realization, no reform.

You are not to think of yourself inferior to anyone - you are not to think of yourself superior to anyone. Discard anything that diminishes you - discard anything that over-glorifies you. You are to step across the rise and fall of the everyday narrowness of society and devote yourself to something greater than personal survival. So I repeat, expand yourself beyond yourself, and the world will be yours.

6.   If You Want Joy

You are the generation corazon, you are the generation assimilation, and it's your accountability that'll resuscitate the heart of humanity. But mark you, generation heart doesn't mean a generation without reason, rather it is the generation that shows the highest sign of reason - generation heart is the generation that realizes warmth and assimilation as the mainspring of life and uses all other elements such as reason, facts and intellect as tools to strengthen the forces of warmth and assimilation.

For example, in such generation science, philosophy, academia, all these exist to lift the whole society, not to serve the whims of the wealthy. Therefore I say, destroy such academia that produces a bunch of morons to serve the rich and privileged.

It is this simple, if you want joy, serve - if you want reform, serve. You are human only when the very title sends a galvanic wave of courage and conscience into the hearts of others. You are human only when any creature bearing that title becomes near and dear to you, no matter their faith, language and culture.

Know this, oneness is civilization, all else is extinction - expansion is civilization, all else is extinction - assimilation is civilization, all else is extinction. What is extinction, one wonders? Is it annihilation of the body? It can be, but extinction of the body is of no consequence, for it is a natural part of life. It is the extinction of the mind that causes all troubles in society.

7. Love First, Reason Later

26

Now the question is, what is mind? Is it merely a matter of intellect? No, it is not, for intellect though crucial, is only a tiny part of everything that constitutes the mind. A mind that solely runs on intellect is no different from a lifeless machine - it may be smart, but that's about all. In fact, pure intellect devoid of emotions and ethics is dangerous.

Let me put this in perspective. Google is one of the smartest algorithms in the world, but can you live your life accompanied solely by google and no human! If the answer is obvious to you, so would the place of smartness in your life as well as in society. Smartness may be a part of life, but it is not life itself.

As I've said in my previous works, it's more important to be kind than right. Let me elaborate a bit further, reason is what helps us eliminate our prejudice, but it's love that makes us want to eliminate our prejudice. Take an eraser for example. You use an eraser to mend a mistake while writing, but the eraser doesn't work until you recognize your mistake and want to correct it.

Prejudice is intrinsic to life in the wild, because life thrives on prejudice in the kingdom of the jungle, but for a species that has cut ties with the jungle, prejudice does more harm than good - as such it is imperative that we stay cautious of our prejudices and choose wisely whether or not to let them drive our behavior.

Reform happens out of intention, and intention happens out of love. Where there is love, there is reform. The being of love doesn't say, give me reform. The being of love says, reform starts with me and ends with me. The being of love doesn't say give me justice. The being of love says, justice starts with me and ends with me.

8. Aşkistani: Citizen of Love
(The Sonnet)

Aşkistani: Citizen of Love
(The Sonnet)

Listen you all peddlers of hate,
Hard as you may blow the horn of tyranny.
To jeopardize all your stone-age stupidity,
You'll always be confronted with an aşkistani.
We won't let your children come to harm,
Nor will we strike you back in vengeance.
But when you vilify the sanctity of human life,
Rest assured we'll restrain you without violence.
Violence may be your childish habit,
You may practice it all you desire.
We are the revolution of conscience,
That incinerates prejudice by sheer willpower.
We are not here to peddle any ideology.
All we ask is come let's be one family.

9.   Smartness is Futile

You don't need to be smart to change the world. You just need to have a sound mind, and a being of love is by nature a being of sound mind. And you know what a sound mind is? A sound mind is one that dreams of a better world and works for a better world while being mindful of the limitations of the present world. We may aim for the ideal if we want to, but we must never lose sight of the present, because the moment we do is the moment we lose touch with reality, and no great future can be built without a firm awareness of the reality we live in.

Now please, do not go into the intellectual debate over the nature of reality, I beg you, for as I've mentioned a million times, reality is a construct of our brain, and as such it is in our hands what kind of reality we want to build. The reality we live in is the construct of our ancestors, and the reality our children will live in, will be the construct of our actions. So throw away the meaningless and rather futile debates of intellect and give yourself wholeheartedly to the making of a humane reality.

Remember, so long as millions starve and live without a roof, I hold every feat of technological achievement a mockery of human life. How come we can spend billions in sending people to MARS and yet cannot take care of the very residents suffering here on earth! What kind of achievement is this? As a scientist I am supposed to be a whole-hearted advocate of space exploration and indeed I am not against it, but what I am against is the reckless pursuit of adventure while our own kind suffers on earth.

Therefore I say, seek neither adventure nor security, seek to alleviate the suffering of others, and you'll have all the joy in the world. In fact, if every child grows up watching their parents lend a hand to those in need, all suffering will fade within a century. Service, service, service – that's the way. And service is not a matter of teaching, it is a matter of realization.

You see, I've never wanted to live as a mortal, I've always wanted to die as an immortal. And the simplest path to immortality is absolute annihilation of the self in the service of others. I could say, serve and you shall receive, but here's the point - if you are serving with the thought of receiving something, then you are refuting your very act of service. Where there is selflessness, there is service, where there is selfishness there is pretense. And pretense may bring shallow publicity, but not real reform.

10. Life Lies in The Soil

Throw away your pretenses - throw away your pride of intellect - throw away all traces of self-aggrandizement. Even the highest philosophy must come down to everyday level of the commoner, otherwise, such philosophy is of no use. That is why I say, if my words don't make sense to the lay people, I've failed. Every word, every thought, every feeling must come down to the soil and work amongst the ordinary people to improve their conditions of everyday life.

It is in the soil that you can realize life. The more distant you get from the soil, the more distant you get from life. Amidst the soil you'll find society - amidst the soil you'll find serenity - amidst the soil you'll find salvation, 'cause what could be more salvific than having people next to us!

You see, power is only power when it lifts the people, without reserve, without sectarianism, without bigotry. And particularly what I must mention is that power and recklessness are a dangerous combination. Power without responsibility can cause more harm than good.

So, all power must be guided by a caring, humane hand, and not by pride or self-interest, be it artificial intelligence, genetic engineering, neurotechnology, or anything else. Our health, our intellect, our resources - if all these only benefit us and do nothing for the people around us, then what's the point of it all!

11. Sonnet of People

Sonnet of People
(The Sonnet)

All is well when there's people with us,
Without 'em life is sugarcane without sugar,
All is meaningful when there's people with us,
Without 'em life is a painting without color.
People are the blood in my veins,
I can breathe without oxygen but not people,
Thus speaks the being called human,
Thus lives the sapiens who's brave and noble.
Community means compatriot unity,
Unity means undivided amity,
Amity means affectionate sanity,
Sanity means serene humanity.
Now one ponders the meaning of humanity.
It means humble and affectionate for eternity.

12. No Need to See Eye to Eye

Life amidst the collective is true life. Individuality in collectivity, collectivity in individuality - that's the principle of a humane society. But mark you, the collective doesn't mean only those you agree with on all matters, the collective means everyone, including those you have difference in opinion. The point is, we don't need to see eye to eye with everyone, we just need to accept the fact that the world is big enough for more than one pair of eyes.

But what you must also keep in mind is, here we are talking about opinions, not discrimination. We must accept differences in opinion, but not inhuman behavior. Discrimination and prejudice are not acceptable in a civilized society, and as such, they must be stood up to by every being of conscience and character - not with violence but with resolve. Hate is not opinion, it is degradation.

Let me elaborate with an example. I've said a million times, I am not a believer, but at the same time, I am not an atheist, because God is nature's antidote to misery and I accept it as such. So, when people take refuge in their personal deity in times of distress, it is not only wrong but downright inhuman to blatantly refute the existence of a supreme being in their face. Therefore acceptance of people's need of faith is the foremost duty of a civilized being.

You'll find fringe groups in every faith, every culture, every nation, who boast the supremacy of their faith, their culture, their nation over others. But you cannot measure an entire community based on the actions of these fringe groups. Stand up to the acts of cultural supremacy, not to a person's right to their culture.

13. Beyond Red and Blue
(The Sonnet)

Beyond Red and Blue
(The Sonnet)

I don't wanna rule no one,
Nor do I wanna prove them wrong.
I don't wanna convert no one,
Nor do I wanna sing the woke song.
My work is with the whole humanity,
No person must be left behind.
Either I'll take them all forward,
Or I'll perish while fixing the great divide.
I don't fathom the red and blue,
You can't make a rainbow with two colors.
If you are really kind and conscientious,
On its own bigotry disappears.
We must rise above all party politika,
Only then will we be the soul of America.

54

14. Beyond Facts and Intellect

Reason has its place – but you must learn where to reason as well as where to keep quiet and accept an irrational act with a smile on your face. Reason must serve warmth, not the other way around. A thousand pounds of facts, intellect and reason are dust in front of one ounce of warmth. Reason can nourish civilization only if it is guided by warmth. You can pour tons and tons of reason into the society, but if you don't have any warmth in your action, all you'll have is a machine driven prehistoric world.

In certain situations the head may take control, but in everyday ordinary living, it's the heart that is to be in control with the head being an aid to the heart. We must not deny head altogether, but as I said, we must know its place. Place your head at the feet of your heart and all will be well, both for you and the society.

The very divide between heart and head disappears once your heart awakens from narrowness. When the heart and head become one, the right place of the head appears on its own. You see, when you have love, you'd naturally know when it's time for reason. When you have love, that very love makes you want to overcome your prejudice.

But the problem is, often we confuse rigidity with love. Take nationalism for example. Lay people as well as learned intellectuals think of nationalism as a love for nation. And loving your nation is truly a civilized act, if it is indeed love, which it never is. Nationalism is not love for one's nation, it's the glorification of one nation while rejecting the shortcomings of that nation, at the expense of the honor of other nations. In short, nationalism is not love, it's selfishness. And as I've said before, selfishness is not civilization, it's plain primitiveness.

15. Love without Growth is No Love

The problem is, love that refutes growth is not love but tyranny. And that's what the so-called love for nation, that is, nationalism does to the fabric of a nation. It tramples all scope for growth while rigidly holding on to the delusion of supremacy or perfection. When you assume you are at your pinnacle, you automatically start going downhill towards imminent disaster, for both yourself as well as the society.

Thus, when you assume your nation needs no improvement, when you assume that your nation is at its absolute best, you are inadvertently burying your nation alive, for a nation that assumes self-proclaimed supremacy is the only inferior nation on earth. A nation is alive only when it grows, constantly discarding its outdated traditions, habits, rituals and assumptions. The same holds true for the individual, as well as the entire world. Refute growth and you refute life.

Let me give you an example. Those who enter America illegally are no different from the pilgrims who founded our country. And white supremacists dehumanize the immigrants as criminals who enter this country illegally in the hope of life and liberty and yet glorify the pilgrims as the founders of America who also entered this land illegally with the same hope! What primitiveness!

In fact, the founders of America were more criminal than modern immigrants – you know why – because the founders of America didn't only enter this land illegally, but after entering they drove the natives out of their own home, whereas all that the immigrants of today want is to have a better life for their family. Now tell me – who are the real criminals?

If the illegal immigrants of today are criminals, so were the illegal immigrants of four hundred years back. And there's the point - you don't see those pilgrims as criminals, for they are the reason you are in this country in the first place, yet you see their present counterparts as criminals, who are forced to flee their country for the same reason the pilgrims fled britain.

This is what nationalism does to a person. It blinds them to the shortcomings embedded in their culture and in their history while making them hateful towards others, particularly those who want to be a part of their culture.

You see, in love there is no place for hate. So, if nationalism was really a form of love, there wouldn't be any hate in it. And though in theory, pompous intellectuals and prehistoric cavemen may define nationalism as love for one's country, the reality is, nationalism is anything but love.

16. No Supremacy in Love

66

A Nationalist doesn't love their country, they only love the high and mighty image of their country, which gives them a sense of supremacy over all other countrymen on earth. That's why you can find elements of supremacy, narrowness and bigotry in the patriotic music of (almost) every country. There is no supremacy in love, and nationalism is but cultural supremacy, therefore, it's no love.

Love means humility, not supremacy - love means kindness, not discrimination - love means acceptance, not prejudice - love means evolution, not rigidity. Where there is real love, that very love brings out the best of humanity in us. And anything that breeds hate and facilitates divisiveness is sheer terrorism. Thus, nationalism is terrorism.

Here I am not advocating for globalism, for nationalism and globalism were both born of ignorance and narrowness. The world doesn't magically become one by replacing one primitive ideology with another - for that to actually happen, you must contain the world in your heart and guard it with your life, as you'd guard your immediate family.

Each day you ought to hold the world up in your hands and say to yourself - it's my world and I'm responsible for it. The joy of lifting the world can't be matched by anything. Mediocre minds discuss people, smart minds discuss ideas, gods discuss less and lift others more. In lifting others, you'll lift yourself up.

But if all you do is care for your own elevation, then at the end of the day, you'll find yourself six feet under. Nationality, religion, color, gender - all these are meaningless - what matters is people, what matters is society, what matters is humanity. You'll know the world has become civilized when terms like nationality, religion, color and gender become archaic.

17. Sonnet of Nationality

Sonnet of Nationality

Nation, nation whatever you are,
Time it is for you to disappear.
Plenty chaos you've caused so far,
Nation, nation now you disappear.
Long ago we lived in tribes,
Slowly we expanded our tiny hives.
Behold ye all the time arrives,
To expand again and merge with all lives.
Nationality keeps the world from peace,
Diplomacy keeps the intention on leash.
Partisanism hides the brotherhood keys,
Self-obsession fans sectarian deeds.
Let the borders trouble the tribal gov,
In our hearts let's rise as citizens of love.

18. When Humanity is Nationality

Expansion is the sign of life. Expand my friend - expand beyond your nation, expand beyond your religion, expand beyond your color, gender and sexuality. Expand beyond the barbaric bounds of tradition and the world will witness the first dawn of civilization in you.

You see, civilization doesn't mean etiquettes, civilization doesn't mean manners, civilization doesn't mean luxuries, civilization means a living, breathing sense of oneness with the whole world. When you feel one with the world, there's no end to what you can achieve, both as an individual and as a collective. Your possibilities are limited only by your imagination.

Be one with the world and live as one world. You see, a nation doesn't exist except in the mind of its people. A nation is only a nation so long as the people believe to belong to that nation. And this belief might have helped our previous generations to survive, but it'll take us no further. Now is the time that we expand our mental imagery of nation and assimilate not a continent, not a hemisphere, but the whole world into it.

Let everyone hear – world is my nation, humanity my nationality. People keep asking me, where do I live? I keep telling them, my physical location is of no significance, for my mind sees no border. I work to serve a world, not a puny tribe from the prehistoric era. So, dare not taint me with your tribal tenets. This is why I said in my last work, leave your crown, your constitution, your scripture outside when you enter my door. And here I add to it further, leave your passport, your diploma, your wallet outside when you enter my door.

But mark you, this doesn't mean I don't have any inclination. Of course I do, for it is impossible for an organic human mind to not foster a sense of inclination towards those from whom it receives most love. As such, my mind has an inclination towards a certain nation as well - it is to my United States of America, for as I've said countless times, she embraced me as her own child when no nation on earth, including the one I was born in, knew I existed.

Similarly you may feel a certain inclination to a certain nation, particularly to the nation you were born or raised in. This inclination is not the problem. Problem occurs when you let this inclination run amok. That's when a healthy national inclination turns into deadly nationalism. So I urge you, for the sake of the security of your children, maintain your inclinations in a way that they don't turn you into a tribal savage.

19. Sonnet of Progress

Sonnet of Progress

Where the nation ends,
There the world begins.
Where the self fades,
There community begins.
Where luxury withers,
There equality begins.
Where biases shrink,
There truth begins.
Where pride dies,
There growth begins.
Where rigidity ends,
There life begins.
Such true life is forever revered.
Prejudice conquered is world conquered.

20. We Are All Born Narrow

Narrowness doesn't need to be taught in school. We are all born with narrowness embedded in our neurons. To unlearn that narrowness will take a lifetime. And it is with this act of unlearning our narrowness, that we shall make our surroundings civilized, that is, human.

Narrowness impairs reform, expansion causes it. Narrowness fosters complacency, narrowness fosters ignorance, and above all narrowness fosters indifference. Indifference is the worst of all sickness. Any creature that aims to rise civilized must cut ties with indifference, allegiance and prejudice. Once you do, you'd realize, there is no such thing as humanitarianism, there's only humanity - there's no such thing as aid, there's only humanity - there's no such thing as inclusion, there's only humanity.

Discard anything that makes you narrow, discard anything that separates you from people, discard anything that impairs your growth. Discard traditions that make you narrow, discard scriptures that make you narrow, discard heritage that makes you narrow, discard culture that makes you narrow, discard constitutions, policies and governments that make you narrow. Expansion is the watchword of life, nay, expansion is life, narrowness is death.

Let me put this into perspective and tell you - universality is life, nationality is death. Nationality is acceptable so long as it is only a matter of paperwork, but the moment it turns into a matter of heartwork, it becomes downright lethal and practically inhuman.

Diplomats continue to sustain a world full of geopolitical conflicts by feeding the population an illusory idea of world peace. You know how they can do that successfully – it's by manipulating people's primitive allegiance to nationality. It is with our desire for ascension from nationality to universality, that we'll ensure actual, real, tangible and practical peace on planet earth.

21. When there is No Sectarianism

The role of diplomacy is not to ensure peace and progress in society, rather it is to look out for the sole benefit of one particular group of people over all others. And such prehistoric system of tribalism, that is diplomacy, is nowhere near capable enough to achieve something civilized and indivisible as world peace. Chisel this into your brain, world peace begins where petty nationalistic identities end.

There is no satellite up in orbit to transmit peace onto the world. Each human is to be a hotspot of peace themselves. I'll say it to you in simple words - nonsectarianism is peace. If even one generation becomes nonsectarian, in thought, in feeling, and in action, all geopolitical conflict will disappear within a century.

But mark you, the world doesn't need some new ideology, such as globalism to replace nationalism, it just needs the humans to behave as humans, beyond and above all sectarian tendencies. No sectarianism, no war - it's that simple.

However, one thing I must make absolutely clear. Without sectarianism, there'll not be any inter-nation war, the kind we have moronically accepted as norm, but there will still be occasional acts of terror, for there'll always be some fringe groups who'll try their best to wreak havoc in an attempt to proclaim themselves as supreme authority of society. But these little inhuman elements can be easily managed by armed intervention.

Here one particular question that may rise is, how can a civilized world have armed intervention! To which I say, if we were living in a fictitious story-book world, we would not need armed intervention, for anything is possible in imagination and fantasy, but we live in an organic world with organic limitations and shortcomings. And one of those shortcomings is that, there'll always be some people who'll be subconsciously driven to the course of violence. And logic does not work on these people, hence rises the need to have some sort of armed forces to keep them in check. Armed forces are there, not to cause violence, but to prevent it, when they appear.

In the absence of sectarianism, what we'll not have however is the constant paranoia that the neighboring nation is going to invade our land in the middle of the night. Such barbarian paranoia is sustained by the prehistoric tenet of nationalistic stupidity, caused by tribal insecurity. You see, ignorance doesn't make a person stupid, aversion to learning and rampant self-absorption do. If you are able to learn with reason at hand and warmth in heart then you'll start to see the foulness of the primitive fantasies, such as nationalism, fundamentalism, elitism, intellectualism, anti-intellectualism and so on.

22. Not Woke, Only Accountable
(A Sonnet)

Not Woke, Only Accountable
(A Sonnet)

I am no teacher but only lover,
I know no philosophy but amity.
I am no writer but only revolution,
I know no politics but serenity.
I am no thinker but only soldier,
I know no science but ascension.
I am no authority but only service,
I know no poetry but inclusion.
I am no humanist but only human,
I know no ideology but oneness.
I am no woke but only accountable,
I know no paradise but acceptance.
Taint not the mind with a puny label.
We are beautiful when we are indivisible.

23. Beyond Intellectualism and Anti-Intellectualism

Some pompous intellectuals may argue, how can intellectualism and anti-intellectualism both be fantasies! To which I say, they are both primitive fantasies, because both proclaim the superiority of extremes - intellectualism proclaims the superiority of intellect, whereas anti-intellectualism denies intellect altogether and proclaims the superiority of emotions devoid of all reason. Thus, both are dangerous for the individual as well as the society, because pure intellect devoid of emotions leads to a cold, mechanical society, whereas pure emotions devoid of intellect lead to a prejudiced society - neither of which fosters a healthy environment for the growth and wellbeing of the human mind.

In fact, nationalism is a form of anti-intellectualism, where the mind denies all reason/intellect that may point to the shortcomings of one's nation. In such anti-intellectualism, if intellect does come to action, it only functions selectively to cherry-pick and then exaggerate the few positive aspects of one's nation. Let me give you an example. I am no democrat or liberal for I despise sectarianism of all sorts, but since reason and assimilation are my watchwords for society, white supremacists see me as their enemy, yet whenever I call upon the vigor to step beyond wokeness as well as rigidity, they most enthusiastically cite me as their defense, omitting the rigidity part of course.

This is what nationalism does. It blinds you to rational arguments that may threaten the integrity of your nation's image, just like fundamentalism blinds you to rational arguments that may threaten the integrity of your religion's image. It's a smoke screen created by the mind and sustained by the mind by means of sentiments which are mostly biases in action, set in motion to protect your barbaric allegiance to your little tribe.

All of this boils down to the primeval drive for self-preservation. What this means is that, if you want growth, harmony and serenity in the world, the first step is to move across the self. Once you move across the self, you are no longer at the mercy of every poppycock whim of the self in the course of self-preservation.

24. Sonnet of Identity

Sonnet of Identity

Tell me O Mississippi,
What is my name?
For I lost my sense of self,
In line of service without gain.
Dear mountains of Blue Ridge,
Where did I come from?
I fathom not the worldly titles,
I deny narrowness as the norm.
Character makes the person,
Not pedigree and tradition.
If I can lift even five lives,
That'll be my highest salvation.
So forget that I asked about my identity.
Service is my culture and my nationality.

25. Meaning of Community

Replace the self with society and self-preservation with collective ascension, and all will be well with the world - if you do not, that is, if the individual psyche continues to live in the foxhole of personal security, then no amount of diplomacy is going to reform the world. Because diplomacy does not reform the world, only oneness does.

Or let me put it in even simpler terms, because the anti-intellectual parts of the society have a tendency to mystify terms like oneness and nonduality, just like the intellectual parts of society have a tendency to take the warmth out of every term. Diplomacy does not reform society only individual sense of community does.

You know what community means - it means compatriot unity - and who are your compatriots - the whole humankind - not the people of a state, a nation or a religion, but the whole wide world. Do you feel that unity with your compatriots my friend? Do you? If you do, then to live without community would mean death for the human in you.

Guns and bombs have more power to take lives than diplomacy and policy have to preserve it. The only thing that has more power than guns and bombs is your everyday sense of community. If you stand strong - if you stand tall, against the everyday discrimination, prejudice and disparities of your surroundings then that very act is the philosopher's stone this worlds needs to change its self-obsessed ways.

They say, ask and you shall receive. And this motto may give you comfort in some imaginary plot of a movie. But the world is no movie. It is real, it is living, it is breathing. And in this real, living, breathing world, all you can do to bring reform is do your part, as unselfishly as possible. Rush to the world without the self, and the world will come rushing to stand by you.

Take nothing as gospel (not even my words), except growth. Grow constantly - incessantly - without any drag, without rigidity, without any reservation whatsoever. Don't let anything come between you and your growth - not your tradition, not your culture, not your heritage, not your religion, not your nationality, not your constitution, not anything whatsoever.

Remember, the world grows when the mind grows, the world falls when the mind falls.

When you grow, you automatically come close to the people, not just to those around you, but also to those thousands of miles away from you. People appear distant when you stop growing. Embrace growth and all distance will disappear making the whole world your family. Growth nourishes love, love fosters growth.

26. The Sufi Sonnet

The Sufi Sonnet*

For your ascension I became a lover,
For your rights I became a revolution.
Ask me not who I am,
Look in my eyes, you'll find your reflection.
Our world is a new world,
The soul of this world is conscience.
Without conscience we all are animals,
March ahead o conscientious with valiance.
There is no other religion but love,
There is no other nationality but humanity.
The story of human is a story of kindness,
If not, life is but an utter futility.
We are all heroes when we are together,
Togetherness forever whether alive or six feet under.

*I wrote this sonnet originally in Turkish, then rewrote in
English, Spanish and Swedish.

27. El Soneto Sufí (Spanish)

116

El Soneto Sufí

Por tu ascension me converti en amante,
Por tus derechos me converti en revolución.
No me preguntes quien soy,
Mírame a los ojos y encontrarás tu reflejo.
Nuestro mundo es un mundo nuevo,
El alma de este mundo es la conciencia.
¡Sin conciencia todos somos animales,
Marcha Adelante, oh concienzudo, con Valentia!
No hay otra religion que el amor,
No hay otra nacionalidad que la humanidad.
La historia del ser humano es una historia de bondad,
Si no, la vida es una absoluta futilidad.
Somos heroes cuando estamos unidos,
Unidos por siempre, ya sea vivos o muertos.

28. Sufi Şiir (Turkish – Original)

Sufi Şiir

Senin ilerlemen için ben aşık oldum,
Senin haklarınız için ben savaşçı oldum.
Sorma canım benim ben kimim,
Gözlerime bak, ben senin yansıman oldum.
Bizim dünyamız yeni bir dünya,
Bu dünyanın ruhu vicdandır.
Vicdan olmadan hepimiz canavarız,
Vicdanla yürü cesur insanlar.
Aşktan başka din yoktur,
İnsanlıktan başka milliyet yok.
İnsan hayati bir merhamet hikayesidir,
Yoksa, bizim hayatımız hayat yok.
Birlikte olduğumuzda biz kahramanlarız,
Birlikte yaşayacağız ve birlikte öleceğiz.

122

29. Sufi Sonett (Swedish)

Sufi Sonett

För din uppstigning blev jag en älskare,
För dina rättigheter blev jag en revolution.
Fråga mig inte vem jag är,
Titta i mina ögon så ser du din reflektion.
Vår värld är en ny värld,
Själen i denna värld är samvete.
Utan samvete är vi alla djur,
Gå framåt, o samvetsgrann med tapperhet.
Det finns ingen annan religion än kärlek,
Mänskligheten är den största nationaliteten.
Människolivet är en berättelse om vänlighet,
Annars, vad är poängen!
Vi är hjältar när vi är tillsammans.
Vi bor tillsammans och vi dör tillsammans.

30. Discard Luxury, Practice Simplicity

When everyone is trying to achieve something for themselves, give up everything you've achieved for the love of others. This is the gist of all my work, nay, this is the gist of my life. And in fact, this is the gist of actual human existence.

Let go of self-obsession - so that the small you can become the world personified. Self-obsession makes the rich richer and poor poorer. Thus, disparities in society continue to flourish in an environment saturated with self-obsession. As a result, the privileged continue to receive all sorts of comfort imaginable while the working class continues to struggle to acquire even the essentials of life.

Remember, there is no chance of welfare in the society, unless the conditions of the working class are improved. Change is not when a billionaire becomes a trillionaire, real societal change is when a construction worker who never passed high school can send their child to college without depending on anyone.

And to achieve this we must discard all luxury from life. Luxury is the enemy of life, for it only produces disparity. Luxury must be banned from human society either by individual initiative, or by government intervention. We don't need a society of abundance, we just need a society of contentment. And to make it happen, we must have a clear sight of our necessities, and those who cannot see for whatever poppycock reason, must be made to see by means of law, that is, through wealth tax.

I ask you here - what are the things that you really need to live a healthy and happy life - think deeply - don't rush to an answer. Do you really need the apple watch? Do you really need to upgrade your phone every time there's a new model? Do you really need a superfast fancy car? Do you? And I am not asking whether you want these or not - I am asking whether you need these.

Remember, a twenty dollar watch shows the same time as a two hundred dollar watch, and also it keeps you healthy, by not conditioning your mind with a ping every few minutes. As for myself, I wear a ten dollar shirt with twenty dollar jeans, shoes and watch, because when you pay less attention to appearance, you can pay more attention to character.

The end of economic disparity will not take place magically out of some fancy diplomatic and political whim. It'll require radical changes to the very mindset of the human population, which will further lead to changes in their lifestyle, that in turn will lead to a society with integrity, stability and character. It is this simple, discard luxury and practice simplicity.

31. Assumption is Corruption

To create a sane society it is imperative to declutter one's life, both mental and physical. In your physical life, remove all elements of luxury, and in your mental life, remove all assumptions. Mark you, luxury doesn't add meaning to your life, if anything, it only takes away all tangible meaning from life, just like assumptions destroy all truth in life.

Most people don't actually live life, for they live in the assumption of life. To actually experience life, you must live rather than assume. Here you may not be the one to blame, for as I've said many times, one of the fundamental functions of the brain is to create assumptions for you to believe in and live in. However, you also do have the brain capacity to be aware of those assumptions and step across them if necessary.

Stop the noise of assumption and you'll hear the music of ascension. Outward assumption is a reflection of inward corruption. Or to put it simply - assumption is corruption, correction is ascension. You see, the joy one receives from learning about a person by holding their hand or by sitting next to them, is insurmountable by the savage acts of assumption. Conversation has life in it, only if it is free from assumptions.

Assumption is a sign of death, not growth. Assumption is the wall, bring it down and the bridge will appear on its own – the bridge to life, the bridge to society, the bridge to humanity.

BIBLIOGRAPHY

Archer M., (2000), Being Human: The Problem of Agency. Cambridge University Press.

Archer M., (2003), Structure, Agency and the Internal Conversation. Cambridge University Press.

Adolphs R (2003) Cognitive neuroscience of human social behaviour. Nature Rev Neurosci 4: 165–178.

Adolphs R, Tranel D, Damasio AR (2003) Dissociable neural systems for recognizing emotions. Brain Cogn 52: 61–69.

Afton, A. D. (1985). Forced copulation as a reproductive strategy of male lesser scaup: A field test of some predictions. - Behaviour 92, p. 146-167.

Allison T, Puce A, McCarthy G. (2000) Social perception from visual cues: role of the STS region. Trends Cogn Sci 4: 267–278.

Andresen, Jensine, and Robert Forman, eds. Cognitive Models and Spiritual Maps. Bowling Green, Ohio: Imprint Academic, 2000.

Ashbrook, James, and Carol Albright. The Humanizing Brain: Where Religion and Neuroscience Meet. Cleveland, OH: Pilgrim Press, 1997.

Azari, Nina, Janpeter Nickel, Gilbert Wunderlich, Michael Niedeggen, Harald Hefter, Lutz Tellmann, Hans Herzog, Petra Stoerig, Dieter Birnbacher, and Rudiger Seitz. "Neural Correlates of Religious Experience." European Journal of Neuroscience 13, no. 8 (2001)

Agar, N. (2004). Liberal eugenics: In defence of human enhancement. London: Blackwell Publishing.

Alteheld, N., Roessler, G., Vobig, M., & Walter, R. (2004). The retina implant new approach to a visual prosthesis. Biomedizinische Technik, 49(4), 99–103.

Antal, A., Nitsche, M. A., Kincses, T. Z., Kruse, W., Hoffmann, K. P., & Paulus, W. (2004a). Facilitation of visuo-motor learning by transcranial direct current stimulation of the motor and extrastriate visual areas in humans. European Journal of Neuroscience, 19(10), 2888–2892.

Bernstein R.J., (1971), Praxis and Action: Contemporary Philosophies of Human Activity. Philadelphia: University of Pennsylvania Press.

Bernstein R.J., (1976), The Restructuring Social and Political Thought.

Bernstein R.J., (1983), Beyond Relativism and Objectivism: Science, Hermeneutics, and Praxis. Philadelphia: University of Pennsylvania Press.

Bernstein R.J., (1986), Philosophical Profiles. Philadelphia: University of Pennsylvania Press.

Bernstein R.J., (1991), New Constellation. Cambridge: MIT Press.

Birkhead, T. R., Johnson, S. D. & Nettleship, D. N. (1985). Extra-pair matings and mate guarding in the common murre Uria aalge. - Anim. Behav. 33, p. 608-619.

Beauregard, Mario, and Vincent Paquette. "Neural Correlates of a Mystical Experience in Carmelite Nuns." Neuroscience Letters 405, no. 3 (2006)

Benson, Herbert. Timeless Healing: The Power and Biology of Belief. New York: Scribner, 1996

Bose, Subhas Chandra. An Indian Pilgrim: An Unfinished Autobiography, Oxford University Press, 1997

Bose, Subhas Chandra. The Indian Struggle 1920-1942, Oxford University Press, 1997

Bogen, J.E.(1995a), 'On the neurophysiology of consciousness: Part I. An overview', Consciousness and Cognition, 4.

Bogen, J.E. (1995b), 'On the neurophysiology of consciousness: Part II. Constraining the semantic problem', Consciousness and Cognition, 4.

Bremner, J. D., R. Soufer, et al. (2001). "Gender differences in cognitive and neural correlates of remembrance of emotional words." Psychopharmacol Bull 35 (3).

Brothers, L. (2002). The social brain: A project for integrating primate behavior and neurophysiology in a new domain. In J. T. Cacioppo et al. (Eds.), Foundations in neuroscience. Cambridge, MA: MIT Press.

Buss, D. D. (2003). Evolutionary Psychology: The New Science of Mind, 2nd ed. New York: Allyn & Bacon.

Buss, D. M. (1989). "Conflict between the sexes: Strategic interference and the evocation of anger and upset." J Pers Soc Psychol 56 (5).

Buss, D. M. (1995). "Psychological sex differences. Origins through sexual selection." Am Psychol 50 (3).

Buss, D. M. (2002). "Review: Human Mate Guarding." Neuro Endocrinol Lett 23 (Suppl 4).

Buss, D. M., and D. P. Schmitt (1993). "Sexual strategies theory: An evolutionary perspective on human mating." Psychol Rev 100 (2).

Blakemore SJ, Decety J (2001) From the perception of action to the understanding of intention. Nature Rev Neurosci 2: 561.

Bruce C, Desimone R, Gross CG (1981) Visual properties of neurons in a polysensory area in superior temporal sulcus of the macaque. J Neurophysiol 46: 369–384.

Buccino G, Vogt S, Ritzl A, Fink GR, Zilles K, Freund HJ, Rizzolatti G (2004) Neural circuits underlying imitation of hand actions: an event related fMRI study. Neuron 42: 323–34.

Colapietro V., (1988), "Human Agency: The Habits of Our Being." Southern Journal of Philosophy, XXVI, 2, pp. 153-68.

Colapietro V., (1992), "Purpose, Power, and Agency." The Monist, 75, 4 (October) pp. 423-44.

Colapietro V., (2004a), "C. S. Peirce's Reclamation of Teleology." Nature in American Philosophy, ed. Jean De Groot (Washington, D.C.: Catholic University Press of America), pp. 88-108.

Colapietro V., (2004b), "Portrait of a Historicist: An Alternative Reading of Peircean Semiotic." Semiotiche, 2/04 [maggio 2004], pp. 49-68.

Colapietro V., (2006), "Engaged Pluralism: Between Alterity and Sociality." The Pragmatic Century: Conversations with Richard J. Bernstein (Albany, NY: SUNY Press), pp. 39-68.

Carey DP, Perrett DI, Oram MW (1997) Recognizing, understanding and reproducing actions. In: Jeannerod M, Grafman J (eds) Handbook of neuropsychology. Vol. 11: Action and cognition. Elsevier, Amsterdam.

Carr L, Iacoboni M, Dubeau MC, Mazziotta JC, Lenzi GL (2003) Neural mechanisms of empathy in humans: a relay from neural systems for imitation to limbic areas. Proc Natl Acad Sci USA 100: 5497–5502.

Changeux JP, Ricoeur P (1998) La nature et la règle. Odile Jacob, Paris.

Chomsky Noam, (2017) Requiem for the American Dream

Chomsky Noam, (2016) Who Rules the World?

Chomsky Noam, (2010) How the World Works

Churchland, P.S. (1986), Neurophilosophy (Cambridge, MA: The MIT Press).

Churchland, P.S. & Ramachandran, V.S. (1993), 'Filling in: Why Dennett is wrong', in Dennett and His Critics: Demystifying Mind, ed. B. Dahlbom (Oxford: Blackwell Scientific Press).

Churchland, P.S., Ramachandran, V.S. & Sejnowski, T.J. (1994), 'A critique of pure vision', in Large- scale Neuronal Theories of the Brain, ed. C. Koch & J.L. Davis (Cambridge, MA: The MIT Press).

Crick, F. (1994), The Astonishing Hypothesis: The Scientific Search for the Soul (New York: Simon and Schuster).

Crick, F. (1996), 'Visual perception: rivalry and consciousness', Nature, 379.

Crick, F. & Koch, C. (1992), 'The problem of consciousness', Scientific American, 267.

Craig AD (2002) How do you feel? Interoception: the sense of the physiological condition of the body. Nature Rev Neurosci 3: 655–666.

Damasio, A (2003a) Looking for Spinoza. Harcourt Inc. Damasio A (2003b) Feeling of emotion and the self. Ann NY Acad Sci 1001: 253–261.

d'Aquili, Eugene. "Senses of Reality in Science and Religion." Zygon 17, no 4 (1982) d'Aquili, Eugene. "The Biopsychological Determinants of Religious Ritual Behavior." Zygon 10, no. 1 (1975)

d'Aquili, Eugene. "The Myth-Ritual Complex: A Biogenetic Structural Analysis." Zygon 18, no. 3 (1983)

d'Aquili, Eugene, and Andrew Newberg. The Mystical Mind: Probing the Biology of Religious Experience. Minneapolis: Fortress Press, 1999.

Daly DD. 1958. Ictal affect. Am J Psychiatry.

Damasio, A. (1994) Descartes' Error: Emotion, Reason and the Human Brain. New York, Putnams.

Damasio, A. (1999) The Feeling of What Happens: Body, Emotion and the Making of Consciousness. London, Heinemann.

Darwin, C. (1859) On the Origin of Species by Means of Natural Selection. London, Murray.

Darwin, C. (1871) The Descent of Man and Selection in Relation to Sex. London, John Murray.

Darwin, C. (1872) The Expression of the Emotions in Man and Animals. London, John Murray; also published 1965, Chicago, University of Chicago Press.

Dawkins, M.S. (1987) Minding and mattering. In C. Blakemore and S. Greenfield (eds) Mindwaves. Oxford, Blackwell, 151-60.

Dawkins, R. (1976) The Selfish Gene. Oxford, Oxford University Press; a new edition, with additional material, was published in 1989.

Dawkins, R. (1986) The Blind Watchmaker. London, Longman.

Di Pellegrino G, Fadiga L, Fogassi L, Gallese V, Rizzolatti G (1992) Understanding motor events: A neurophysiological study. Exp Brain Res 91: 176–80.

Deikman, A.J. (2000) A functional approach to mysticism. Journal of Consciousness Studies 7(11-12), 75-91.

Delmonte, M.M. (1987) Personality and meditation. In M. West (ed.) The Psychology of Meditation. Oxford, Clarendon Press, 118-32.

Dennett, D.C. (1988) Quining qualia. In A.J. Marcel and E. Bisiach (eds) Consciousness in Contemporary Science. Oxford, Oxford University Press, 42-77.

Dennett, D.C. (1991) Consciousness Explained. Boston, MA, and London, Little, Brown and Co.

Dennett, D.C. (1995a) Darwin's Dangerous Idea. London, Penguin.

Dennett, D.C. (1995b) The unimagined preposterousness of zombies. Journal of Consciousness Studies 2(4), 322-6.

Dennett, D.C. (1995c) Cog: steps towards consciousness in robots. In T. Metzinger (ed.) Conscious Experience. Thorverton, Devon, Imprint Academic, 471-87.

Dennett, D.C. (1996a) Facing backwards on the problem of consciousness. Journal of Consciousness Studies 3(1), 4-6.

Dennett, D.C. (1996b) Kinds of Minds: Towards an Understanding of Consciousness. London, Weidenfeld & Nicolson.

Dennett, D.C. (1997) An exchange with Daniel Dennett. In J. Searle (ed.) The Mystery of Consciousness. New York, New York Review of Books, 115-19.

Dennett, D.C. (1998) The myth of double transduction. In S.R. Hameroff, A.W. Kaszniak and A. C. Scott (eds)

Toward a Science of Consciousness: The Second Tucson Discussions and Debates. Cambridge, MA, MIT Press, 97-107.

Dennett, D.C. (1998b) Brainchildren: Essays on Designing Minds. Cambridge, MA, MIT Press.

Dennett, D.C. (2001) The fantasy of first person science. Debate with D. Chalmers, Northwestern University, Evanston, IL, February 2001.

Dennett, D.C. (2003) Freedom Evolves. New York, Penguin.

Dennett, D.C. and Kinsbourne, M. (1992) Time and the observer: the where and when of consciousness in the brain. Behavioral and Brain Sciences 15, 183-247, including commentaries and authors' responses.

Dewey J., (1911 [1977]), "Epistemological Realism: The Alleged Ubiquity of the Knowledge Relation."

Journal of Philosophy, VIII, 20 (September 28, 1911).

Dewhurst, Kenneth, and A. W. Beard. "Sudden Religious Conversions in Temporal Lobe Epilepsy." British Journal of Psychiatry 117 (1970)

Dewhurst K, Beard AW. Sudden religious conversions in temporal lobe epilepsy. 1970 Epilepsy Behav 2003

Devinsky O, Lai G. Spirituality and religion in epilepsy. Epilepsy Behav 2008.

Devinsky, O., Morrell, MJ, Vogt, BA. (1995) 'Contribution of anterior cingulate cortex to behavior', Brain, 118.

Douglas Stone A., Chapter 24, The Indian Comet, in the book Einstein and the Quantum, Princeton University Press, Princeton, New Jersey, 2013.

E. Horvitz, "One Hundred Year Study on Artificial Intelligence: Reflections and Framing," ed: Stanford University, 2014.

Einstein A. (1925). "Quantentheorie des einatomigen idealen Gases". Sitzungsberichte der Preussischen Akademie der Wissenschaften.

Eckhart Meister, Selected Writings

Egidi R., ed. (1999), "Von Wright and 'Dante's Dream': Stages in a Philosophical Pilgrim's Progress", in In Search of a New Humanism: the Philosophy of G.H. von Wright, ed. by R. Egidi, Kluwer, Dordrecht.

Fadiga L, Fogassi L, Pavesi G, Rizzolatti G (1995) Motor facilitation during action observation: a magnetic stimulation study. J Neurophysiol 73: 2608–2611.

Fogassi L, Gallese V, Fadiga L, Rizzolatti G (1998) Neurons responding to the sight of goal directed hand/arm actions in the parietal area PF (7b) of the macaque monkey. Soc Neurosci Abs 24:257.5.

Frith U, Frith CD (2003) Development and neurophysiology of mentalizing. Philos Trans R Soc Lond B Biol Sci 358: 459.

Farah, M.J. (1989), 'The neural basis of mental imagery', Trends in Neurosciences, 10.

Finlay BL, Darlington RB (1995) Linked regularities in the development and evolution of mammalian brains. Science 268.

Freud, S. "The Interpretation of Dreams", 1900

Freud, S. "Selected papers on hysteria and other psychoneuroses" Journal of Nervous and Mental Disease 1909.

Freud, S. "The Origin and Development of Psychoanalysis", 1910

Freud, S. "Psychopathology of everyday life", 1914

Freud, S. "Beyond the Pleasure Principle", 1920

Frith, C.D. & Dolan, R.J. (1997), 'Abnormal beliefs: Delusions and memory', Paper presented at the May, 1997, Harvard Conference on Memory and Belief.

Gay, Volney, ed. Neuroscience and Religion. Plymouth, UK: Lexington Books, 2009.

Gazzaniga, M. S. (1985). The social brain. New York: Basic Books.

Gazzaniga, M.S. (1993), 'Brain mechanisms and conscious experience', Ciba Foundation Symposium, 174.

Geschwind N. "Behavioural changes in temporal lobe epilepsy". Psychol Med. 1979.

Gellhorn, E., Kiely, W.F. "Mystical states of consciousness: neurophysiological and clinical aspects." J Nerv Ment Dis. 1972;154:399-405.

Gilbert SL, Dobyns WB, Lahn BT (2005) Genetic links between brain development and brain evolution. Nat Rev Genet 6.

Gray JA. The Psychology of Fear and Stress. 2nd ed. New York, NY: Cambridge University Press; 1988.

Gloor, P. (1992), 'Amygdala and temporal lobe epilepsy', in The Amygdala: Neurobiological Aspects of Emotion, Memory and Mental Dysfunction, ed J.P. Aggleton (New York: Wiley-Liss).

Greenspan, S. I. and S. G. Shanker (2004). The first idea: How symbols, language, and intelligence evolved from our early primate ancestors to modern humans. Cambridge, MA: Da Capo Press.

Grady, D. (1993), 'The vision thing: Mainly in the brain', Discover, June.

Gallagher HL, Frith CD (2003) Functional imaging of 'theory of mind'. Trends Cogn Sci 7: 77.

Gallese V, Fogassi L, Fadiga L, Rizzolatti G (2002) Action representation and the inferior parietal lobule. In: Prinz W, Hommel B (eds) Attention & Performance XIX. Common mechanisms in perception and action. Oxford University Press, Oxford.

Gallese V, Keysers C, Rizzolatti G (2004) A unifying view of the basis of social cognition. Trends Cogn Sci 8: 396–403.

Gangitano M, Mottaghy FM, Pascual-Leone A (2001) Phase specific modulation of cortical motor output during movement observation. NeuroReport 12: 1489–1492.

Gangitano M, Mottaghy FM, Pascual-Leone A (2004) Modulation of premotor mirror neuron activity during observation of unpredictable grasping movements. Eur J Neurosci 20: 2193– 2202.

Goldman AI, Sripada CS (2004) Simulationist models of face-based emotion recognition. Cognition 94: 193–213.

Grèzes J, Costes N, Decety J (1998) Top-down effect of strategy on the perception of human biological motion: a PET investigation. Cogn Neuropsychol 15: 553–582.

Grèzes J, Armony JL, Rowe J, Passingham RE (2003) Activations related to "mirror" and "canonical" neurones in the human brain: an fMRI study. Neuroimage 18: 928–937.

Gross CG, Rocha-Miranda CE, Bender DB (1972) Visual properties of neurons in the inferotemporal cortex of the macaque. J Neurophysiol 35: 96–111.

Hari R, Forss N, Avikainen S, Kirveskari S, Salenius S, Rizzolatti G

(1998) Activation of human primary motor cortex during action observation: a neuromagnetic study. Proc. Natl Acad Sci USA 95: 15061–15065.

Hardy, G. H. (1940). Ramanujan. Cambridge: Cambridge University Press.

Hall, Daniel, Keith Meador, and Harold Koenig. "Measuring Religiousness in Health Research: Review and Critique." Journal of Religion and Health 47, no. 2 (2008)

Harris, Sam, Jonas Kaplan, Ashley Curiel, Susan Bookheimer, Marco Iacoboni, and Mark Cohen. "The Neural Correlates of Religious and Nonreligious Belief." PLoS One 4, no. 10 (October 1, 2009)

Halgren, E. (1992), 'Emotional neurophysiology of the amygdala within the context of human cognition', in The Amygdala:

Neurobiological Aspects of Emotion, Memory and Mental Dysfunction, ed J.P. Aggleton (New York: Wiley-Liss).

Halligan PW, Fink GR, Marshal JC, Vallar G. 2003. Spatial cognition: evidence from visual neglect. Trends Cogn Sci.

Handbook of Emotions, Edited by Michael Lewis, Jeannette M. Haviland-Jones, and Lisa Feldman Barrett, The Guilford Press; 3rd edition (2010).

Hameroff, S.R. and Penrose, R. (1996) Conscious events as orchestrated space-time selections. Journal of Consciousness Studies 3(1), 36-53; also reprinted in J. Shear (ed.) (1997) Explaining Consciousness-The Hard Problem. Cambridge, MA, MIT Press, 177-95.

Harding, D.E. (1961) On Having no Head: Zen and the Re-Discovery of the Obvious. London, Buddhist Society.

Hardy, A. (1979) The Spiritual Nature of Man: A Study of Contemporary Religious Experience. Oxford, Clarendon Press.

Harre, R. and Gillett, G. (1994) The Discursive Mind. Thousand Oaks, CA, Sage.

Haugeland, J. (ed.) (1997) Mind Design II: Philosophy, Psychology, Artificial Intelligence. Cambridge, MA, MIT Press.

Hauser, M.D. (2000) Wild Minds: What Animals Really Think. New York, Henry Holt and Co.; London, Penguin.

Hebb, D.O. (1949) The Organization of Behavior. New York, Wiley.

Helmholtz, H.L.F. von (1856-67) Treatise on Physiological Optics.

Hess, EH (1975) "The role of pupil size in communication," Scientific American, 233(5), 110–12.

Heyes, C.M. (1998) Theory of mind in nonhuman primates. Behavioral and Brain Sciences 21, 101-48; with commentaries.

Heyes, C.M. and Galef, B.G. (eds) (1996) Social Learning in Animals: The Roots of Culture. San Diego, CA, Academic Press.

Hilgard, E.R. (1986) Divided Consciousness: Multiple Controls in Human Thought and Action. New York, Wiley.

Hitler, Adolf. Mein Kampf, 1925

Hodgson, R. (1891) A case of double consciousness. Proceedings of the Society for Psychical Research 7, 221-58.

Hofstadter, D.R. and Dennett, D.C. (eds) (1981) The Mind's I: Fantasies and Reflections on Self and Soul. London, Penguin.

Holland, J. (ed.) (2001) Ecstasy: The Complete Guide: A Comprehensive Look at the Risks and Benefits of MDMA. Rochester, VT, Park Street Press.

Holmes, D.S. (1987) The influence of meditation versus rest on physiological arousal. In M. West (ed.) The Psychology of Meditation. Oxford, Clarendon Press, 81-103.

Holmstrom, David. 1992, Christian Science Monitor

Holt, J. (1999) Blindsight in debates about qualia. Journal of Consciousness Studies 6(5), 54-71.

Holloway RL (1996) Evolution of the human brain. In: Lock A, Peters CR (eds) Handbook of human symbolic evolution. Oxford University Press, Oxford

Iacoboni M, Woods RP, Brass M, Bekkering H, Mazziotta JC, Rizzolatti G (1999) Cortical mechanisms of human imitation. Science 286: 2526–2528.

Iacoboni M, Koski LM, Brass M, Bekkering H, Woods RP, Dubeau MC, Mazziotta JC, Rizzolatti G (2001) Reafferent copies of imitated actions in the right superior temporal cortex. Proc Natl Acad Sci USA 98: 13995–13999.

Jeannerod M (1988) The neural and behavioural organization of goal-directed movements. Clarendon Press, Oxford.

Johnson-Frey SH, Maloof FR, Newman-Norlund R, Farrer C, Inati S, Grafton ST (2003) Actions or hand-objects interactions? Human inferior frontal cortex and action observation. Neuron 39: 1053–1058.

Jackson, F. (1982) Epiphenomenal qualia. Philosophical Quarterly 32, 127-36.

James, W. (1890) The Principles of Psychology (2 volumes). London, Macmillan.

James, W. (1902) The Varieties of Religious Experience: A Study in Human Nature. New York and London, Longmans, Green and Co.

Jansen, K. (2001) Ketamine: Dreams and Realities. Sarasota, FL, Multidisciplinary Association for Psychedelic Studies.

Jay, M. (ed.) (1999) Artificial Paradises: A Drugs Reader. London, Penguin.

Jaynes, J. (1976) The Origin of Consciousness in the Breakdown of the Bicameral Mind. New York, Houghton Mifflin.

Johnson, M.K. and Raye, C.L. (1981) Reality monitoring. Psychological Review 88, 67-85.

Kadim I, Mahgoub O, Baqir S et al. (2015) Cultured meat from muscle stem cells: a review of challenges and prospects. J Integr Agr 14: 222–233

Kandel, E. R. In Search of Memory: The Emergence of a New Science of Mind, W. W. Norton & Company (2007).

Kandel E. R. Schwartz JH, Jessel TM. Principles of neural sciences. New York; McGraw Hill, 2000.

Kanwisher, N. (2001) Neural events and perceptual awareness. Cognition 79, 89-113; also reprinted inS. Dehaene (ed.) The Cognitive Neuroscience of Consciousness. Cambridge, MA, MIT Press, 89-113.

Karn, K. and Hayhoe, M. (2000) Memory representations guide targeting eye movements in a natural task. Visual Cognition 7, 673-703.

Kennedy, H., & Dehay, C. (1988). Functional implications of the anatomical organization of the callosal projections of visual areas V1 and V2 in the macaque monkey. Behav. Brain Res., 29, 225–236.

Kentridge, R.W. and Heywood, C.A. (1999) The status of blindsight. Journal of Consciousness Studies 6(5), 3-11.

Kihlstrom, J.F. (1996) Perception without awareness of what is perceived, learning without awareness of what is learned. In M. Velmans (ed.) The Science of Consciousness. London, Routledge, 23-46.

Kosslyn, S.M. (1980) Image and Mind. Cambridge, MA, Harvard University Press.

Kosslyn, S.M. (1988) Aspects of a cognitive neuroscience of mental imagery. Science 240, 1621-6.

Kinsbourne, M. (1995), 'The intralaminar thalamic nucleii', Consciousness and Cognition, 4.

Kjaer, Troels, Camilla Bertelsen, Paola Piccini, David Brooks, Jorgen Alving, and Hans Lou. "Increased Dopamine Tone during Meditation- Induced Change of Consciousness." Cognitive Brain Research 13, no. 2 (April 2002)

Kölmel HW. 1985. Complex visual hallucinations in the hemianopic field. J Neurol Neurosurg Psychiatry.

Koenig, Harold. "Research on Religion, Spirituality, and Mental Health: A Review." Canadian Journal of Psychiatry 54, no. 5 (May 2009)

Koenig, Harold, ed. Handbook of Religion and Mental Health. San Diego, CA: Academic Press, 1998

Kraepelin E. Psychiatry: A Textbook for Students and Physicians. New York, NY: Science History Publications; 1990.

Lauglin, Charles, John McManus, and Eugene d'Aquili. Brain, Symbol, and Experience. 2nd ed. New York: Columbia University Press, 1992

Lakoff, G. and M. Johnson (1999). Philosophy in the flesh. Basic Books: New York.

LeDoux, J. E. (1996). The emotional brain. New York: Simon & Schuster.

LeDoux, J.E. (1992), 'Emotion and the amygdala', in The Amygdala: Neurobiological Aspects of Emo- tion, Memory and Mental Dysfunction, ed J.P. Aggleton (New York: Wiley-Liss).

Levin, D.T. and Simons, D.J. (1997) Failure to detect changes to attended objects in motion pictures. Psychonomic Bulletin and Review 4, 501-6.

Levine,J. (1983) Materialism and qualia: the explanatory gap. Pacific Philosophical Quarterly 64, 354-61.

Levine,J. (2001) Purple Haze: The Puzzle of Consciousness. New York, Oxford University Press. Levine, S. (1979) A Gradual Awakening. New York, Doubleday.

Levinson, B.W. (1965) States of awareness during general anaesthesia. British Journal of Anaesthesia 37, 544-6.

Lewicki, P., Czyzewska, M. and Hoffman, H. (1987) Unconscious acquisition of complex procedural knowledge. Journal of Experimental Psychology: Learning, Memory and Cognition 13, 523-30.

Lewicki, P., Hill, T. and Bizot, E. (1988) Acquisition of procedural knowledge about a pattern of stimuli that cannot be articulated. Cognitive Psychology 20, 24-37.

Lewicki, P., Hill, T. and Czyzewska, M. (1992) Nonconscious acquisition of information. American Psychologist 47, 796-801.

Manthey S, Schubotz RI, von Cramon DY (2003). Premotor cortex in observing erroneous action: an fMRI study. Brain Res Cogn Brain Res 15: 296–307.

Mesulam MM, Mufson EJ (1982) Insula of the old world monkey. III: Efferent cortical output and comments on function. J Comp Neurol 212: 38–52.

Naskar, Abhijit. "Homo: A Brief History of Consciousness", 2015

Naskar, Abhijit. "What is Mind?", 2016

Naskar, Abhijit. "Love, God & Neurons: Memoir of A Scientist who found himself by getting lost", 2016

Naskar, Abhijit. "Principia Humanitas", 2017

Naskar, Abhijit. "We Are All Black: A Treatise on Racism", 2017

Naskar, Abhijit. "Either Civilized or Phobic: A Treatise on Homosexuality", 2017

Naskar, Abhijit. "I Am The Thread: My Mission", 2017

Naskar, Abhijit. "The Bengal Tigress: A Treatise on Gender Equality", 2017

Naskar, Abhijit. "Morality Absolute", 2017

Naskar, Abhijit. "Build Bridges not Walls: In the name of Americana", 2018

Naskar, Abhijit. "Fabric of Humanity", 2018

Naskar, Abhijit. "Lives To Serve Before I Sleep", 2019

Naskar, Abhijit. "Citizens of Peace: Beyond the Savagery of Sovereignty", 2019

Naskar, Abhijit. "The Constitution of The United Peoples of Earth", 2019

Naskar, Abhijit. "Neurons Giveth, Neurons Taketh Away | Abhijit Naskar | TEDxIIMRanchi", 2019 https://www.youtube.com/watch?v=B NX-Q0ySm80

Naskar, Abhijit. "Mission Reality", 2019

Naskar, Abhijit. "Operation Justice: To Make A Society That Needs No Law", 2019

Naskar, Abhijit. "Every Generation Needs Caretakers: The Gospel of Patriotism", 2020

Naskar, Abhijit. "Hurricane Humans: Give me accountability, I'll give you peace", 2020

Naskar, Abhijit. "Revolution Indomable", 2020

Naskar, Abhijit. "Servitude is Sanctitude", 2020

Naskar, Abhijit. "Good Scientist: When Science and Service Combine", 2020

Newberg, Andrew, and Jeremy Iversen. "The Neural Basis of the Complex Mental Task of Meditation: Neurotransmitter and Neurochemical

Considerations." Medical Hypotheses 61, no. 2 (2003).

Newberg, Andrew. "How God Changes Your Brain: An Introduction to Jewish Neurotheology", CCAR Journal: The Reform Jewish Quarterly, Winter 2016.

Newberg, Andrew, and Stephanie Newberg. "A Neuropsychological Perspective on Spiritual Development." In Handbook of Spiritual Development in Childhood and Adolescence, edited by Eugene Roehlkepartain, Pamela King, Linda Wagener, and Peter Benson. London: Sage Publications, Inc., 2005

Newberg, Andrew. "The Neurotheology Link An Intersection Between Spirituality and Health", Alternative and Complimentary Therapies, Vol 21 No 1, February 2015.

Newberg, Andrew, Nancy Wintering, Dharma Khalsa, Hannah

Roggenkamp, and Mark Waldman. "Meditation Effects on Cognitive Function and Cerebral Blood Flow in Subjects with Memory Loss: A Preliminary Study." Journal of Alzheimer's Disease 20, no. 2 (2010)

Nash, M. (1995), 'Glimpses of the mind', Time.

Nesse RM. Proximate and evolutionary studies of anxiety, stress and depression: synergy at the interface. Neurosci Biobehav Rev. 1999;23:895-903.

Nicolelis, Miguel. (2011) "Beyond Boundaries: The New Neuroscience of Connecting Brains with Machines--- and How It Will Change Our Lives", Times Books

O'Hara, K. and Scutt, T. (1996) There is no hard problem of consciousness. Journal of Consciousness Studies 3(4), 290-302, reprinted in J. Shear (ed.)

(1997) Explaining Consciousness. Cambridge, MA, MIT Press, 69-82.

O'Regan, J.K. (1992) Solving the "real" mysteries of visual perception: the world as an outside memory. Canadian Journal of Psychology 46, 461-88.

O'Regan, J.K. and Noe, A. (2001) A sensorimotor account of vision and visual consciousness. Behavioral and Brain Sciences 24(5), 883-917.

O'Regan, J.K., Rensink, R.A. and Clark,].]. (1999) Change-blindness as a result of "mudsplashes." Nature 398, 34.

Ornstein, R.E. (1977) The Psychology of Consciousness (2nd edn). New York, Harcourt.

Ornstein, R.E. (1986) The Psychology of Consciousness (3rd edn). New York, Pehguin.

Ornstein, R.E. (1992) The Evolution of Consciousness. New York, Touchstone.

Penfield W, Faulk ME (1955) The insula: further observations on its function. Brain 78: 445– 470.

Penrose, R. (1994), Shadows of the Mind (Oxford: Oxford University Press).

Penrose, R. (1989), The Emperor's New Mind: Concerning Computers, Minds and The Laws of Physics (Oxford: Oxford University Press).

Persinger, "'I would kill in God's name' role of sex, weekly church attendance, report of a religious experience and limbic lability" Perceptual and Motor Skills 1997.

Persinger "Experimental simulation of the God experience" Neurotheology 2003.

Persinger, M. A. (1993b). Personality changes following brain injury as a grief response to the loss of sense of self: Phenomenological themes as indices of local lability and neurocognitive restructuring as psycho- therapy. Psychological Reports, 72

Persinger, Corradini, Clement, Keaney, et al "Neurotheology and its convergence with neuroquantology" NeuroQuantology 2010.

Persinger, Koren and St-Pierre "The electromagnetic induction of mystical and altered states within the laboratory" Journal of Consciousness Exploration and Research 2010.

Persinger "Case report: A prototypical spontaneous 'sensed presence' of a sentient being and concomitant electroencephalographic activity in the clinical laboratory" Neurocase 2008.

Persinger and Saroka "Potential production of Hughlings Jackson's "parasitic consciousness" by physiologically-patterned weak transcerebral magnetic fields: QEEG and source localization" Epilepsy & Behavior 28 (2013).

Persinger. "The neuropsychiatry of paranormal experiences". J Neuropsychiatry Clin Neurosci 2001.

Persinger. "Neuropsychological bases of god beliefs", New York: Praeger, 1987

Persinger. "Temporal lobe epileptic signs and correlative behaviors displayed by normal populations", Journal of General Psychology, 1986

Perry BD, Pollard R. Homeostasis, stress, trauma, and adaptation. A neurodevelopmental view of childhood trauma. Child Adolesc Psychiatr Clin N Am. 1998;7:33.

Paré, D. & Llinás, R. (1995), 'Conscious and preconscious processes as seen from the standpoint of sleep-waking cycle neurophysiology', Neuropsychologia, 33.

Phillips ML, Young AW, Senior C, Brammer M, Andrew C, Calder AJ, Bullmore ET, Perrett DI, Rowland D, Williams SC, Gray JA, David AS (1997) A specific neural substrate for perceiving facial expressions of disgust. Nature 389: 495–498.

Phillips ML, Young AW, Scott SK, Calder AJ, Andrew C, Giampietro V, Williams SC, Bullmore ET, Brammer M, Gray JA (1998) Neural responses to facial and vocal expressions of fear and disgust. Proc R Soc Lond B Biol Sci 265: 1809–1817.

Puce A, Perrett D (2003) Electrophysiological and brain imaging of biological motion. Philosoph Trans Royal Soc Lond, Series B, 358: 435–445.

Ramachandran VS. Behavioral and magnetoencephalographic correlates of plasticity in the adult human brain. Proc Natl Acad Sci USA 1993; 90: 10413–20.

Ramachandran VS. Phantom limbs, neglect syndromes, repressed memories, and Freudian psychology. Int Rev Neurobiol 1994; 37: 291–333.

Ramachandran VS. Plasticity and functional recovery in neurology. Clin Med 2005; 5: 368–73.

Ramachandran VS, Hirstein W. The perception of phantom limbs. The D. O. Hebb lecture. Brain 1998; 121: 1603–30.

Ramachandran VS, Rogers-Ramachandran D, Cobb S. Touching the phantom limb. Nature 1995; 377: 489–90.

Ramachandran VS, Rogers-Ramachandran D. Phantom limbs and

neural plasticity. Arch Neurol 2000; 57: 317–20.

Ramachandran VS, Rogers-Ramachandran D. It's all done with mirrors. Sci Am Mind 2007; 18: 16–9.

Ramachandran VS, Rogers-Ramachandran D. Sensations referred to a patient's phantom arm from another subjects intact arm: perceptual correlates of mirror neurons. Med Hypotheses 2008; 70: 1233–4.

Ramachandran VS, Rogers-Ramachandran D, Stewart M. Perceptual correlates of massive cortical reorganization. Science 1992; 258: 1159–60.

Rizzolatti G, Craighero L (2004) The mirror-neuron system. Annu Rev Neurosci 27: 169–192.

Rizzolatti G, Fogassi L, Gallese V (2001) Neurophysiological mechanisms underlying the understanding and imitation of action. Nature Rev Neurosci 2:661–670.

Rock I, Victor J. Vision and touch: an experimentally created conflict between the two senses. Science 1964; 143: 594–6.

Rose´n B, Lundborg G. Training with a mirror in rehabilitation of the hand. Scand J Plast Reconstr Surg Hand Surg 2005; 39: 104–8.

Royet JP, Plailly J, Delon-Martin C, Kareken DA, Segebarth C (2003) fMRI of emotional responses to odors: influence of hedonic valence and judgment, handedness, and gender. Neuroimage 20: 713–728.

Rozin R Haidt J and McCauley CR (2000) Disgust. In: Lewis M, Haviland-Jones JM (eds) Handbook of Emotion. 2nd Edition. Guilford Press, New York, pp 637–653.

Saxe R, Carey S, Kanwisher N (2004) Understanding other minds: linking developmental psychology and functional neuroimaging. Annu Rev Psychol 55: 87–124.

S. J. Russell and P. Norvig, Artificial intelligence: a modern approach (3rd edition): Prentice Hall, 2009.

Singer T, Seymour B, O'Doherty J, Kaube H, Dolan RJ, Frith CD (2004) Empathy for pain involves the affective but not the sensory components of pain. Science 303: 1157–1162.

Smith A (1759) The theory of moral sentiments (ed. 1976). Clarendon Press, Oxford.

Sprengelmeyer R, Rausch M, Eysel UT, Przuntek H (1998) Neural structures associated with recognition of facial expressions of basic emotions Proc R Soc Lond B Biol Sci 265: 1927–1931.

Strafella AP, Paus T (2000) Modulation of cortical excitability during action observation: a transcranial magnetic stimulation study. NeuroReport 11: 2289–2292.

Schilling, Vincent. 2017, indian country today

Stein, Stephen K. 2017, The Sea in World History: Exploration, Travel, and Trade

Simonsen R (2015) Eating for the future: veganism and the challenge of in vitro meat. In: Stapleton P, Byers A (Hg). Biopolitics and utopia. Palgrave Macmillan, New York (2015), S 167–190

Tanaka K (1996) Inferotemporal cortex and object vision. Ann Rev Neurosci. 19: 109–140.

Tesla N. "My Inventions", 1919

T. R. Society, "Machine learning: the power and promise of computers that learn by example," ed. The Royal Society, 2017.

Tomasello M, Call J (1997) Primate cognition. Oxford University Press, Oxford.

Tremblay C, Robert M, Pascual-Leone A, Lepore F, Nguyen DK, Carmant L, Bouthillier A, Theoret H (2004) Action observation and execution: intracranial recordings in a human subject. Neurology. 63: 937–938.

Umilta MA, Kohler E, Gallese V, Fogassi L, Fadiga L, Keysers C, Rizzolatti G (2001) "I know what you are doing": a neurophysiological study. Neuron 32: 91–101.

9 798504 314693